How to Avoid a Half Marathon Meltdown: 10 Things You Need to Know to Make Sure Your First Half Marathon Isn't Your Last!

by Scott O. Morton

© 2018 by LERK Publishing, LLC. All rights reserved.

LERK Publishing, LLC

Cover design: LERK Publishing, LLC

ISBN **978-1-947010-33-8**

Follow me on Facebook and Twitter:

Twitter: @BeginR2FinishR

Facebook: facebook.com/BeginnerToFinisher/

Website: www.halfmarathonforbeginners.com

Email: scottmorton@halfmarathonforbeginners.com

To my brother, Kevin.

How to Avoid a Half Marathon Meltdown

Medical Disclaimer

The information in this book is meant to supplement, not replace, proper half marathon training. A sport involving speed, equipment, balance and environmental factors, and running, will involve some inherent risk. The authors and publisher advise readers to take full responsibility for their safety and know their limits. Before practicing the skills described in this book, be sure that your equipment is well maintained, and do not take risks beyond your level of experience, aptitude, training, and comfort level.

If you have sports related injuries, I highly suggest that you talk to a medical professional to determine if you are fit enough to endure running. Not seeking medical advice could further exacerbate an existing injury. I am not a legal or medical professional, nor am I offering any type of legal or medical advice. One last time, if you're injured or have medical conditions that prevent you from taking on a rigorous running training program, please seek the opinion of a licensed physician before participating in any physical training. While the training required for a half marathon is not nearly as difficult as the training for a full marathon, it will still push both your mental and physical capabilities.

Other Books by Scott O. Morton

Beginner to Finisher Series:

Book 1: *Why New Runners Fail: 26 Ultimate Tips You Should Know Before You Start Running!*

Book 2: *5K Fury: 10 Proven Steps to Get You to the Finish Line in 9 weeks or less!*

Book 3: *10K Titan: Push Beyond the 5K in 6 Weeks or Less!*

Book 4: *Beginner's Guide to Half Marathons: A Simple Step-By-Step Solution to Get You to the Finish Line in 12 Weeks!*

Book 5: *Long Run Hacks: 20 Ultimate Tips to Help You Push Through Hard Runs!*

Book 6: *How to Avoid a Half Marathon Meltdown: 10 Things You Need to Know to Make Sure Your First Half Marathon Isn't Your Last!*

Book 7: *Marathon Machine - Breakthrough Your Running Barrier in 18 weeks and Conquer Your Dream! (COMING SOON)*

Supercharge Your Walking Life:

Book 1: *42,000 Steps: 100 simple ways to maximize your daily step count!*

Book 2: *Supercharged Walking: 20 Simple Methods to Help You Level Up Your Stride!*

Book 3: *Walkathon - The Ultimate Guide to Walking a 5K, 10K, Half Marathon, or Marathon!*

Table of Contents

Why I Wrote This Book

It seems that there are quite a number of people that want to make the leap from running 5Ks or 10Ks into half marathons and beyond. From the feedback I have received over the past year a lot of people struggle with the mental side of running. Shaping and strengthening your mind will help make your longer runs more manageable (notice that I didn't say easier).

Running is a challenge in itself. For every mile that we run our bodies become more and more exhausted. Our mind is continuously finding new ways to avert our progress and throw us off track. I've run over 50 races and I promise you that the mental side of running is always there. However, you can learn a few techniques in this book that might very well help you strengthen your inner coach and quell your inner critic.

To all your future races I wish you the best.

No Shortcuts Exist

Why does it take so long to train for a half marathon?

When you're a beginner runner training for your first half marathon the upper end of training schedules can look a little intimidating. Most half marathon training schedules, especially for new runners, fall between 10 weeks and 16 weeks in total duration. Why does it take so long to train for a half marathon if you're a new runner? The most important reason why it takes so long to prepare for a half marathon is that new runner's bodies aren't conditioned to run for a duration of 2 to 4 hours. If you slowly increment your total mileage on a week by week basis you can and will prepare your body for the 13.1-mile distance.

No shortcuts exist.

If you don't believe me, go ask a marathon runner. Your body has to learn how to store glycogen. The basic process of building up your glycogen store looks something like this:

- run a long duration run of X miles. (x being the number of miles needed for the week).
- your muscles break down and rebuild within 24-48 hours.
- The ability for your legs to store more glycogen slowly increases on a week to week basis.
- Food and rest help refill your newly expanded energy stores

so that you can run a little further each week (this is why rest is important).

- Repeat the steps above while increasing your long run.

Does it really take at least 12 weeks to train for 13.1 miles?

No, not if you're an experienced runner. Let's say that I run 3 miles 4 times a week. Could I go out and run a half marathon at any given time without long distance training? Yes, however, I would be putting my body at extreme risk of injury and possibly worse. There is a reason why there are thousands of half marathon training plans on the Internet. The truth of the matter is that most half marathon training plans have a "buffer" baked into the training plan. This buffer allows for the possibility of sickness or minor injury where you can't run the long run for that week.

What happens when you get sick or injured and miss an important run during a half marathon training cycle? If for some reason you get sick and can't make a long distance run (for a half marathon anything above 9 miles), as long as you complete at least three runs at and above 9 miles, then you should be able to finish a half marathon. This by no means is an excuse or reason to slack off and not run all your long distance runs. 3 long runs at or above 9 miles would be the bare minimum training I would recommend to complete a half marathon without injury.

Get Plenty of Rest

Rest/Recovery

Rest and recovery are sometimes understated. During the 70s, runners quiet often ran every single day without a break. Eventually, if you run every single day with no breaks, you will sustain some type of injury. Running is an impact sport. Your body is continuously pounding the pavement mile after mile impacting your ligaments, joints, muscles, and bones with each stride.

Since the 1970s, study after study has been done on injury prevention for runners. One of the top reasons for a running relating injury to occur was due to lack of rest or recovery. Also, in the top of the list was running while already injured, you would be surprised at how many people still run while they are injured. By exploring the physical and mental sides of rest, as well as rest during your training schedule and on race day, we can help shed some light on the area.

Rest - The Physical Side

When you run any distance you are breaking down muscles in your body. The muscles in your legs need 24 to 48 hours to rebuild. If you continuously run, every day, your muscles won't build as efficiently if you just took a few rest days per week. On your rest days you don't have to be completely idle, just don't run. On one of your rest days during the week try to perform some type of cross training such as weightlifting.

Rest - The Mental Side

Have you ever woken up and knew that you needed to log a run for the day, but you were just too groggy? Well, more than likely, the reason you didn't want to run was because of a lack of rest. I know because I've been there before.

Eyes burning, mouth wide open from continuously yawning, as I glance at my run schedule for that day. And of course, it's a long run that I need to tackle to the extent of 10 miles. My 1 year old chose not to sleep the night prior to this scheduled long run. Instead of pushing through with the run, I chose to put off the run for the next day. Sometimes, getting rest is more important than a run. You can always reschedule a run, but if your body is only running at 25% of capacity, it's probably better to put your running shoes away for the day.

Rest During Training

If you're a first time half marathon runner or a fairly new runner, I suggest having at least one rest day that you perform a minimal amount of exercise. The best day for a complete rest would be the day after your long runs. The long run should be the most vigorous and exhausting run of the week. During this rest day, your body is rebuilding your muscles and training your body to increase your glycogen stores allowing your body to increase it's running mileage week after week.

Rest Before Race Day

New half marathon runners might find it difficult to sleep well the night before a race. Usually the night before a race you are nervous and anxious and you tend to toss and turn all night long. I wish I could tell you that after you've run a couple half marathons that your rest will improve the night before a race, but in my case, it hasn't. I've run 8 half marathons and a countless number of 5Ks, and I still don't get adequate sleep the night before a race. I usually get good sleep two nights before the race and of course the night after I finish a race.

If you want to have a successful half marathon race, I urge you to make sure that you have calculated enough rest into your training schedule.

Hydration

During your half marathon training, hydration plays a key role in helping you finish the race. Are there some runners that can run an entire half marathon race without hydrating during the race, yes. You can train your body to run the entire distance with only the water you drink prior to the race. For first time half marathon runners, this isn't feasible. Here is a breakdown of some key areas during your half marathon training that you need to consider for hydration purposes.

Hydrating during your base runs

A base run is a run that is designed to help build your base to sustain greater lengths of runs. At the beginning level during your half marathon training, base runs consist of miles anywhere from 2 to 6 miles (most of these are 3 and 4 miles). When I trained for my first half marathon I drank about 12 oz of water prior to my base runs and nothing else during the run. After I completed the base mile run, I drank something to replace my sodium loss, such as G2 Gatorade.

Hydrating during your long runs

During my long runs, anything in excess of 6 miles for me, I wore a CamelBak Hydration Pack. I filled up my 2-liter pack only halfway since I didn't need 2 liters of water. I would train myself to drink water only on the mile marker. Another strategy commonly used is to drink a few sips of water whenever you feel thirsty, that way you don't have to over think it. If you don't plan on using a hydration pack for your actual race, but instead want to carry a handheld sports bottle, you can perform the same type of sipping every mile or whenever you're thirsty.

If you tend to sweat a lot, you might need to increase your intake of fluids or some type of electrolyte sports drink. Each person's amount of fluid needs varies from individual to individual. You might have to experiment a little bit to figure out just how much water your body needs. In my half marathon guide, I provide a simple strategy to determine how much water you will need for your half marathon race.

Hydration on race day

Leading up to the start of the race try to drink at least 12 oz (1/3 of a liter) of water. If you're racing with your own handheld water bottles, hydration belt, or hydration pack then you should know how much water to pack and how much to drink on race day. If you're racing without any hydration help then you need to scout out the locations of the water stations along your race course. Some water stations might have gaps as long as 3 miles between each other. In this case, I would slow down to a walk and drink a cup of water at each water station. If you've been sweating a lot grab a cup full of sports drink at the same time.

Don't drink too much prior to your race

If you've drunk too much water prior to your race, your stomach will be sloshing around making you feel uncomfortable. If this is the case try to use the restroom and relieve yourself.

Bonus

If you're properly hydrated and actually don't need any more water at any particular water station along your route then grab a cup and dump it over your head. The volunteers will get a good laugh and you will get to cool down for a few minutes. If you really want the volunteers to laugh throw it on your racing buddy instead. I've done this many times during my racing history.

Fueling

How Much Fuel?

For absolute beginners, determining when to fuel and how much to fuel during training is always a tough one to nail down. One of the main reasons that beginners are lost when it comes to fueling is due to all of the different opinions floating around. Supplemental companies want you to fuel as much as your body will assimilate per hour which is roughly between 250 - 350 calories depending on your metabolism. Some super elite runners, which are extremely rare individuals, manage to train their bodies to run on zero extra fuel except for their pre-race meal and water during the run. For the beginner and average runner, the odds are against them if they don't fuel during training for a marathon. Yes, I'm sure it's been done, but at what cost to your body?

Do I really need to fuel for a half marathon?

This is a matter of preference. I think the jury is out and I think it's 50/50 on whether or not to fuel for a half marathon. If you don't ever plan on running a marathon, then you might consider and even try to run the half marathon without fueling. If you plan on moving on to bigger races then it would be in your best interest to learn to fuel at a lower level because the marathon will require some type of fuel for you to finish the race. My take away is that if you are a seasoned marathon runner then you probably will not need to fuel for the half marathon race. A simple breakfast with enough calories would suffice. Again, it's a matter of preference. However, if this is your first half marathon, I would lean towards fueling.

Runs shorter than 60 minutes

New runners that run for less than 60 minutes, which is roughly between 4 and 7 miles, only need water during their run. There is no need to eat a gel pack for runs lasting less than 60 minutes. Your energy will not be depleted and you should be able to easily complete the run

Runs between 60 and 90 minutes

This is a gray area for new runners. My best advice is that if you are training for a half marathon or a marathon and your runs are lasting between the 60 and 90-minute marker, then you should go ahead and be training your body to accept the gels that you will be using in the race. If you are just running to run and not really "training" for a race then you can get away with just drinking water and not fueling. Each individual runner will have to experiment with this gray area. For myself, I don't fuel during my long runs which last less than 90 minutes which is the equivalent of about 8 - 9 miles. The key here is to listen to your body and if you are starting to feel fatigued go ahead and fuel past 60 minutes.

Runs greater than 90 minutes

If you're training for a half marathon or marathon I would recommend that during your long runs you use energy gels that you will be eating in the race. Don't forget that training is the time to experiment with your gels. Gels have different flavors as well as different ingredients. For the most part, energy gels are 100 calories and offer both potassium and sodium. Some runners like the gels with a caffeine boost while others don't. Some runners, including myself, suck on shot blocks in between their dose of energy gels during a race. Each shot block is about 30 calories.

Training = Testing Time

The best and worst part about training is that you get to test out your fueling. As a runner, I know first hand, that each runner is different and the number of fuel requirements varies from runner to runner. Some runners like to take a gel right before a half marathon race and marathon race while others don't eat their first gel until 45 minutes into the race.

My Half Marathon Fueling Strategy

Fuels: GU Energy Gels (variety pack), Clif Shot Blocks - variety pack, or Salted Watermelon

I have tried all of the GU flavors and I'm lucky in that my stomach has never disagreed with any GU flavor, yet. If I had to pick a favorite I would go with Salted Watermelon and Orange Creme.

Weight: 220 lbs   Height: 6' 3"

Pre-Race Meal (as soon as I get up): 4 pieces of cinnamon bread, 2 scrambled eggs, 1/2 cup of oatmeal and peanut butter. (600-700 calories)

No Pre Race Gel - I might eat a small snack like an energy bar.

30 minutes - 1 gel (drink water with gel)

45 minutes - 1 shot block

60 minutes - 1 gel (drink water with gel)

1 hour 15 minutes - 1 shot block

90 minutes - 1 gel (drink water with gel)

1 hour 45 minutes - 1 shot block

2 hours - 1 gel (drink water with gel)

2 hours 15 minutes - 1 shot block (if needed - I normally finish under 2:15)

The total amount of calories I consume during a half marathon race is about 500 calories.

Every Runner is Different

The biggest take away is that every runner is different. You need to experiment to find what works best for you. Remeber, sometimes running out of energy on a long run doesn't really have to do with fueling, but could be from lack of adequate sleep or feeling under the weather. All runners at all age levels suffer from lousy runs - I promise. The key is to find out what works best for your body to give you optimal racing conditions.

Main Goal

Don't make a common first time half marathon mistake

New half marathon runners dive into their training plans with varying degrees of objectives and goals. Some runners are trying to finish the race with a predetermined pace and time while others are running the half marathon to support a worthy cause. Whatever the reasons are for running a half marathon don't lose sight of your main objective. If you're a first-time half marathon runner then your main goal should be simple and easily accomplished. A great goal to carry with you during your half marathon training is to simply finish the race.

Your racing against yourself and no one else

Ok, if you're competitive, then this paragraph might make you wince a little bit, in fact, you might just skip to the next paragraph. First of all, I'm competitive so I totally understand why you want to race everyone around you. My purpose for writing these articles and posts is to make it as simple as possible for the average person to complete a half marathon. Even if the runner's goal is to finish the race by walking the entire half marathon. Making your goal easy to attain for your first half marathon will help ensure you that you will finish the race.

Other goals to consider

Not only do you want to finish the race, but my guess is that you'll probably want to finish the race injury free. To help guarantee that you finish a half marathon race injury free, you need to practice listening to your body. If you're injured or your muscles ache, make sure and take the time to roll out your muscles with a foam roller or trigger ball. If you're injured for only a week. The total capacity of your ability to store glycogen will only slightly drop. If you find your body injured for more than 2 weeks, your ability to store glycogen hasn't quite fallen off a cliff so you could still finish your half marathon training plan. If your injury has you out for 3 weeks plus I would suggest restarting your training program when you are healed with no apparent sustained injury.

Don't train when injured

I know I'm repeating myself a little bit, but I want to drill this into your head. I want you to have a long-running career and not cut short by running when you shouldn't be running. I have had my fair share of aches and pains during my many half marathon training cycles. During my sixth half marathon training cycle, I was having issues with my arch in my right foot where I would experience an erratic sharp pain in my foot followed by slight cramping. The cramping occurred during my longer runs of 6 miles plus.

I listened to my body and took about 9 days off from running. Instead of running, I walked every day and used a foot roller to help work out any facial tissue issues around my arch in my foot. I also spent some extra time in the gym lifting weights and performing foot and leg stretches. After a nine-day break from running, I was no longer experiencing the sharp pains or aches.

How do I know if I'm injured

The way I approach running aches, pains, and/or injuries, is like this.

Mild stiffness, or slight aches or cramps: slow down my pace to a walk if I have to. If necessary I will stop and stretch out my stiffness or cramps

Medium aches (slightly harder to judge): this pain is usually a sudden pain experienced during running, I would slow down to a walk and then call it quits for 2-3 days and then ease back into my training cycle.

Pains that require you to stop everything immediately: I haven't experienced this before, but what I've been told from other runners, this could come in the form of ACL, MCL tears, severe cramping, extreme heel pain from **plantar fasciitis.** Obviously, if the injury is severe enough you will want to stop running and consult with a sports doctor ASAP.

Run within your own means

Every runner has different pain and injury thresholds. It's important to listen to your body while running and if you need to slow down your pace or stop running altogether for the next couple of days you might be better off long-term. I have been fortunate and not had any debilitating running injuries to date so far. I use an extremely cautious approach to running. If I have aches other than cramping I take my legs for a test drive before racking up the miles for the day. Also, remember to always perform a proper cool down and stretch after you've run for the day, especially after you longer runs.

Backup Plan

Develop a strategy to finish your first half marathon

As you begin your training for your half marathon, consider developing a strategy for finishing your race. If you plan on walking the entire half marathon course then your only strategy will be to walk it at a fast pace so that you can finish the race before the cut off time. If you're planning on running the entire race then you need to spend some time during training developing a backup strategy just in case.

Backup Plan B

During a few of your long runs during your training, consider working on a backup plan in case you can't run the entire race. There are several strategies floating around on the internet. Here are a few of them that you can test out.

Ralking and Wunning Intervals

Yes, you read that right, Ralking and Wunning. I didn't misspell the words above. Ralking is a majority of walking with occasional running intervals mixed in. Wunning is a majority of Running with occasional walking intervals mixed in. Let's take a look at a few detailed strategies of both forms of exercise.

Time Intervals

For some runners, basing your running and walking interval on time is much easier to gauge, especially if you're wearing a smartwatch. Time interval walking/running looks like this:

Run 9 minutes, walk 1 minute

Run 8 minutes, walk 2 minutes

Run 7 minutes, walk 3 minutes

Run 6 minutes, walk 4 minutes

Run 5 minutes, walk 5 minutes

Run 4 minutes, walk 1 minute, run 4 minutes, walk 1 minute

Run 3 minutes, walk 2 minutes, run 3 minutes, walk 2 minutes

Distance intervals

For other runners, using distance markers during a half marathon race might be the easier way to know when to take a short walking break.

Mile markers

At every mile marker simply walk for 60 seconds or whatever time you need to take a quick break. Alternatively, you could just as easily walk for 1/10 of a mile/km to catch a break as well.

Water/aid stations

Another alternative strategy is to only take a short walking break through every water/aid station. If you can get a hold of the course map during your training cycle, the race creators will normally map out the location of the water aid stations. If you know the distances based on the map then you can take your break at the same distance as each water station you can then take a break at the same distance as your water aid station during your long run training.

Walking through the water aid stations also allow your body to drink water while walking instead of running. Drinking out of the small cups while running is another acquired skill altogether. I found that folding the cup at the top and then drinking from the folded end much easier.

Geographic intervals

Another type of strategy I've used several times on a race course is walking each hill encountered. Here are three different strategies that stand out:

Walk the Hills on the way up

If the race course has a lot of hills, walking each hill could very well help conserve more energy for the latter part of the race. At the top, you go ahead and run down the other side of the hill.

Walk the Hills on the way down

Similar to walking up the hills but reversed. If you want to speed up your hill running then run up the hills and rest your legs by walking down the other side of the hill.

Run half way up each hill

This involves a mixed approach when hills are encountered on the course. Some runners will pick up their pace about 1/10 of a mile/km from a hill and push hard up the hill until they run out of steam and slow to a walk. At that point, they stop running and finish the rest of the hill by walking.

A Hybrid approach

You can incorporate all or some of these approaches into your half marathon course strategy. I tend to walk for about 60 seconds during each water aid station and then walk up the big hills. Most noteworthy, by implementing these two strategies I converse some of my energy for the last 3 miles of a half marathon race.

In conclusion, Each runner is different and some runners will choose not to walk at all during their half marathon. The key is to figure out what strategies work best for you.

Runner's Mindset

Fear - The mental side of running.

Getting past the fear of running 13.1 miles is one of the biggest hurdles of completing a half marathon. The trick is to adopt a runner's mindset. I'm going to let you in on a big secret that helped me get past my fear of having to run 13.1 miles. Most first-time runners don't run the entire 13.1 miles. Wow, what a secret. It's true. The super athletes and other runners trying to beat their personal best records might very well run the entire race. I've completed eight half marathons and one full marathon. Most runners, at a minimum, walk through the water aid stations along the course. Once I realized that you don't have to run the entire distance, the fear of running a half marathon vanished, instantly. My mind had found a chink in the armor.

Believe in yourself

Different nutrition guides, shoe strategies, running miles per week, etc. Among all these differences, there is one common thing agreed upon by almost all runners - You have to believe in yourself and believe that you are a runner. Without this firmly ingrained in your head, you won't make it past mile nine, and you won't make it to the finish line. I'm not telling you this to discourage you. I'm telling you this to prepare you for the mental battle of running.

Learn to like discomfort

Whenever we take on something new that will challenge both our physical capabilities and mental strength, we enter into a state of discomfort. In this state of discomfort, or discomfort zone, nothing is yet routine and we're having to learn new things. While your body and mind are in this zone experiencing new habits and routines, your body and mind are in a state of personal growth. Without pushing ourselves in our own lives we become comfortable and safe (comfort zone), yet we don't experience a great increase in personal growth.

While in the state of discomfort, your mind will continuously try to get you to come back to the comfort zone. If you stick with a training plan and follow someone's step by step advice, you can make extraordinary things happen. By using affirmations and visual exercises I've learned to help push myself through any discomfort zone I've come across.

Disillusion zone

One word of caution when stepping into discomfort zones is to not overstep into a zone of disillusionment. In other words, don't bite off more than you can chew. For example, let's say that I am thirty years old and I have never participated in any sports whatsoever. I decide that I want to run a marathon in under fours hours and be trained in the next 15 weeks. This is clearly jumping way too far into the discomfort zone and this will quickly lead to injury, quitting, or both. Know thyself and your capabilities. In this above scenario, a much better goal would be too simply state that I want to be able to run a 5K without walking in the next 16 weeks. While it's great to shoot for the stars, this goal is much more attainable than the previous goal.

Affirmations/Mantras

I first learned about affirmations from a book written by Jack Canfield called, _The Success Principles._ I had just turned forty and was wondering if there was anything I could do to help further my career along and obtain more personal growth. Affirmations, are simple positive statements that help you focus on an end result or state of being. Some examples could include, _I am a runner,_ or, _I will cross the half marathon finish-line._ Affirmations can be anything from any part of your life. The key is to repeat them multiple times per day to yourself. Mantras, are usually words or sounds used in meditation. Mantras tend to me much shorter in length, for instances, _run, run, run,_ or, d_on't stop running._ Technically mantras and affirmations are used interchangeably. If you haven't used affirmations before, try it out.

Visualizing success

Another key way to keep your mind focused and break through mental barriers is to visualize your success. Whatever you want to accomplish try to visualize yourself completing the task. If one of your goals is to complete a first time half marathon, then close your eyes and visualize how you will feel when you have accomplished the feat. Another way you can implement visualization is to cut out a picture of yourself and place it in between a finish line photo. Place that photo on your fridge as a reminder of your goal. If you keep repeating visualization exercises and repeating daily affirmations, you will slowly start to feel a little bit better in the discomfort zone.

The Long Run

The Long Run

The long run is the most important run during your half marathon training. If you neglect your scheduled long runs your body will not be properly conditioned to finish a first time half marathon. I know this may sound obvious but the whole reasons why you train for 10 weeks plus is to allow your body to store glycogen to be used to propel you to the finish line. By incrementally adding on 1 mile per week, you should be close to a 12-mile long run by the end of your training schedule. Three key things you must do so that your long runs are working to your advantage on race day are: Fuel, Finish, and Recover.

Fueling

There have been recent trends and studies suggesting that Ketogenic Dieting is a better alternative to use when training for long distance running. The studies actually have been showing that towards the end of each of their running sessions, the ketogenic dieting had a slight decrease in performance while the carb dieting had a slightly better performance. Ketogenic dieting is training your body to burn a higher percentage of fat stores (which our bodies have plenty of) versus using your glycogen stores (carbs) for energy. You can read the article here.

Regardless if your fueling with carbs or fats, you need to use your long runs as mini race training sessions. Initiate the same routines on every long run. Here is a mini checklist of things to consider for your long run training session:

Layout your clothes the night before, shoes, mp3 players,

glasses, headbands, whatever you need on your run

Wake up and practice eating your pre-race meal (this could be anywhere from 400 to 800 calories and might include cinnamon bread, bagel with peanut butter, a few eggs, hash browns)

Consider how long your run is for. Bring the appropriate number of gel packs that you need for that particular run (anything less than 60 minutes/6 miles I don't fuel beyond my pre-race meal, this is a matter of personal preference)

Post run - eat a light snack and replace your fluid loss during the run

In my post, I discuss fueling in more detail, How to avoid a half marathon meltdown - Part 4 of 10.

Finishing

Unless you become injured to the point were sharp pains are stabbing you in your legs or obviously something more serious, always try to finish your long runs. This means that if you have a 9-mile run and at mile 7.5 you want to throw in the towel and stop - don't quit. Instead revert back to a walk-run strategy, for example, walk 2 minutes, run 3minutes, etc. If you can't physically run anymore then walk out the remaining miles. Your body needs to cool down anyway, so finishing your last couple of miles by walking is occasionally ok, just don't make a habit out of it.

Recovering

Both before and after your long run you need to rest and recover. The day before your long run needs to be kept to a nonimpact cardio day. This will help to allow your muscles to rebuild for 24 hours prior to you depleting all of your glycogen stores during your long run. After your long run, you need to have a recovery day to help rebuild your body. Your legs need to rebuild your muscles that you broke down during your run. Also, you need to eat nutritious meals to help rebuild your glycogen stores.

Core Values

Core Values

Why do some of go on to finish a half marathon training schedule and physical race and others don't? If we took a look at two different runners both the age of 45 with both of them having the same physical capability, no injuries, and same exercise capacity why is it then possible for one to finish a race and another not succeed? There are many different ideas and reasons why this could happen. If we narrowed the differences between each runner even further such as neither runner would become sick. Also, both have the same amount of time to allocate to exercise. The only thing left comes down to a person's core values. These are values that help each person every day make the decisions that they make.

If we decide today, that in 12 weeks we are going to complete our first half marathon, our present state changes from a static state to a growth state of mind. We are leaving our current state of security and certainty to a state of growth and uncertainty. Uncertainty, can be anything from "will I finish the race?" or "Am I a strong enough runner to finish a half marathon?" Also, this can come from your past, for instance, a past coach telling you that, "you weren't fit enough to run." If some of these past experiences haunt you then you will need to spend a little time with your future self.

Past Self

Have ever been laughed at because you've done something extremely silly which left you feeling embarrassed? Has someone told you that you weren't good enough to do something? Have you told yourself that you couldn't do something because of some circumstance? Odds are you've experienced all three of these things. These past experiences can creep up on you especially when you're trying to take a new direction in life (growth). The key is to reprogram yourself with new beliefs about what you can do and when you will do it. This is where affirmations can help out tremendously. Simply telling yourself twice a day that "I will finish a half marathon race on <insert date>." Eventually, if you keep repeating these affirmations, you will believe it and hopefully turn this into a success.

Present Self

While you're out on your runs training for a half marathon, try to be in the present. Feel your feet touch the ground, concentrate on your breathing, relax your shoulders a bit and live in the moment. I guess this is one of running's biggest draws for me. I get to take a break from the world and get in touch with my inner present thoughts and enjoy feeling alive. We spend so much of our day to day routine dwelling on the past and also seeking out the future that we need to bring ourselves back to the present. Meditation, although this isn't for everybody, can help you concentrate on the here and now and rid yourself of past and future thoughts that lead nowhere.

Future Self

By practicing various forms of visualization you help put your present self in a future state. When I started training for my first half marathon I followed this routine before every long run:

Perform about 5 minutes of dynamic stretching (knee hikes, side gallops, etc)

Close my eyes and visualize myself finishing my long run for the day. I would reach out and try to picture how it will feel to finish the half marathon race.

I would practice taking some deep breaths and try to clear my mind.

By making visualization or mediation a daily routine you are continually making a connection between your present self and future self. Eventually, these two will merge and you will have accomplished your task that your future self-visualized.

Inner Coach vs. Inner Critic

YOU Vs. YOU

If you made it through all of my posts on, *How to Avoid a Half Marathon Meltdown,* you've probably come to realize that running is almost as much a mental battle as it is a physical one. Every day we get up and we try to progress in some area or aspect of our life. When we throw in additional factors that aren't part of our normal routine, it takes an extra amount of exertion to push ourselves to perform those non-routine tasks. That's why I can't stress enough that you need to create a few affirmations that you can repeat daily. By repeating these daily affirmations you can help quell the inner critic.

"...the worst enemy you can meet will always be yourself"
- Friedrich Nietzsche

Inner Critic

While you've been reading this, it's possible that your inner critic has paid you a visit. Your inner critic may very well have even asked you a question such as, "Do you really have time to read this post?" We all have an inner critic that critiques our every thought and move. Yes, he serves a really good purpose especially for survival and from making huge mistakes we've made in the past.

However, your inner critic also listens to external sources and is programmed by what he hears. These can be things you heard from teachers or parents when you were growing up. Even though I've published over 15 books in multiple languages, it's still tough writing the next book. I still to this day have my inner critic tell me things like, "I won't succeed as a writer" or "I just don't feel like writing today." When I hear these things like this, I have to wake up the inner coach to come to fight off the inner critic.

Inner Coach

"Keep going, don't stop, you only have 3 miles left." This is the inner coach that is there to help push you when you need an extra kick. The inner coach doesn't magically appear for everyone. Some individuals have to help train the inner coach with things such as meditation, visualization, and affirmations. If your inner critic is punching the lights out of your coach you need to start performing one of the three suggestions to help train your inner coach. Pick one or two affirmations that you want to get started with. If you have too many they will overbear you and tend to stress you out. Remember that affirmations can be for any part of your life. Here are a few more examples:

I will increase my sales this year by 50%.

l will run a marathon by <insert date>

I will run 3 miles today.

I will learn to surf by July 2018 (this was actually one of mine which I accomplished)

The sky is the limit. Try to keep them measurable with a time frame attached.

What's Next?

Depending on where you are in your training one of the books below might serve your needs:

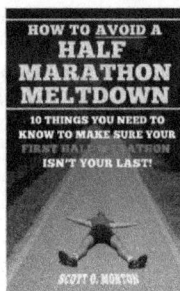

I NEED YOUR HELP!

Thanks for reading! If you've enjoyed this book, please leave me a 5-star gleaming review by simply stating one or two sentences describing what you liked best about the book. Other shoppers on rely on ratings so that it can save them valuable time when shopping for new books. I take the time to read each review. Your help and support are very much appreciated.

Click here to review book

If you've just finished a race and you want someone to tell, send me an email. I would be delighted to hear from you.

Follow me on Facebook and Twitter:

Twitter: @BeginR2FinishR

Facebook: facebook.com/BeginnerToFinisher/

Website: www.halfmarathonforbeginners.com

Email: scottmorton@halfmarathonforbeginners.com

Special sneak peek of, *Why New Runners Fail: 26 Ultimate Tips You Should Know Before You Start Running,* (Book #1 in the Series Beginner to Finisher)

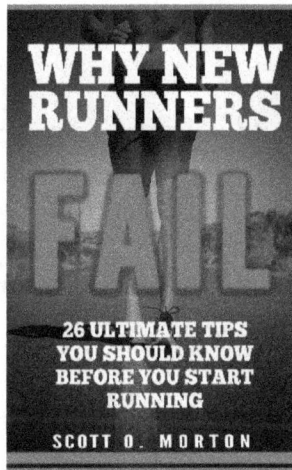

Not Running Enough

Running too little will not allow your body to get used to a training schedule. For example, let's say that you only run two days a week—let's pick Monday and Thursday–to run. Each session consists of 1 mile running followed by 1 mile of walking.

Negatives:

Your body isn't getting used to running.

You might be more susceptible to injury because your body isn't able to rebuild and reuse the muscles quickly enough. It's almost like your body is forgetting how to run between workouts.

You won't be able to progress much further than your training mileage.

Inadequate running makes the mental struggle harder on the mind. Your mind and body think they are being reset after each run session and are not learning the habit of running.

Positives:

You are exercising.

I don't think that you should ever drop below an absolute minimum of three days running/walking. I prefer at least four days of running. If you decide to run a maximum of three days, I highly suggest that you skip every other day (see below).

Three days of training

Monday	Tuesday	Wednesday	Thursday	Friday	Saturday	Sunday
Run	Rest	Run	Rest	Run	Rest	Walk

Four days of training (Preferred)

Monday	Tuesday	Wednesday	Thursday	Friday	Saturday	Sunday
Run	Run	Rest	Run	Rest	Run	Walk

Action Steps

Running too little makes it tougher on your body than having a normal running schedule.

Don't run less than 3 times a week if you want to progress in the sport of running.

Special sneak peek of, *5K Fury: 10 Proven Steps to Get You to the Finish Line in 9 weeks or less!*

(Book #2 in the Series Beginner to Finisher)

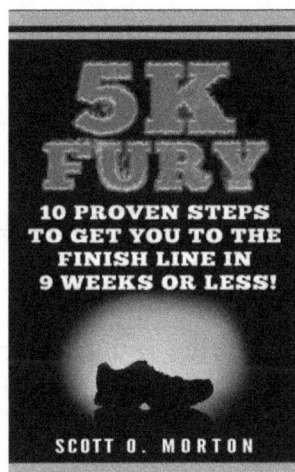

Motivation

Why do some people finish marathons and other don't? I believe it comes down to self-motivation and determination. Self-motivation, while probably the strongest of any other form of motivation, is not the only source of motivation. There are several different types of motivation. Three types of motivation that I believe are the most influential come from social media, running partners and yourself.

Social Media

Social media can help keep you focused and motivated by your circle of friends. You can post running times and screen shots of your runs to social media to let your circle of friends comment and cheer you on. Social media will help perk you up when you have a day that you just don't feel like running.

Running Partners

Running partners are the next best thing to yourself keeping you motivated. They train with you. They give you feedback. They help you stay on pace. They push you when you have no more energy. Partners also help you stay accountable for following through with your goal. One caveat to a running partner is that if they lack self-motivation, they aren't going to be of much help motivating you.

Yourself

Self-motivation is by far the most powerful source of motivation. You know yourself better than anyone else. You are custom to knowing how your mind and body work. If you don't feel like running one day, tell yourself that you will just run a half a mile. After you run a half mile, tell yourself that you will just run one mile. By pushing yourself just a little bit, you can trick your mind into running.

Your motivation could be to get healthy and fit. Also, you could be motivated just to prove to yourself that you can finish a 5K or to donate to a worthy cause. Whatever the motivation is, you and only you will finish the race.

Touch here to purchase.

5K Fury: 10 Proven Steps to Get You to the Finish Line in 9 weeks or less!

For a special sneak peek of,

Special sneak peek of,

10K Titan: Push Beyond the 5K in 6 Weeks or Less!,

(Book #3 in the Series Beginner to Finisher

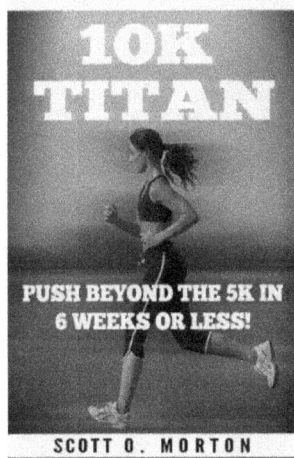

Fear of Running Far

New runners fear running past the distance of a 5K (3.1 miles). Why do we fear running longer distances? Here is a list of some of the reasons we might tell ourselves as to why we don't attempt to run past 3.1 miles:

I'm not a runner.

I'm not a long distance runner.

I fear that my body might not make it.

I fear I might get injured.

There is noway I can run that far and for that long.

I can't run that far.

I'm too overweight.

I'm too out of shape.

I'm too old.

People might make fun of me if I tell them I'm training for a 10K.

The list goes well beyond some of the reasons listed above as to why we might be holding ourself back from running the distance of a 10K. There are too many "I can't"s above. You have to shake loose the phrase, "I can't." That phrase poisons your mind with disbelief even before you get started.

Special sneak peek of,

Beginner's Guide to Half Marathons: A Simple Step-By-Step Solution to Get You to the Finish Line in 12 Weeks!

(Book #4 in the Series Beginner to Finisher)

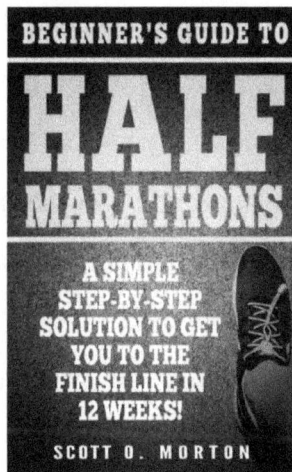

Beginner's Guide to Half Marathons has become an **Amazon #1 Bestseller.**

The runner's mindset. Getting past the fear of running 13.1 miles is one of the biggest hurdles of completing a half marathon. I'm going to let you in on a big secret that helped me get past my fear of having to run 13.1 miles. The secret is that most runners don't run the entire 13.1 miles. Wow, what a secret. It's true. The super athletes and other runners trying to beat their personal best records might very well run the entire race. However, I have completed three half marathons and one full marathon, and the majority of runners will walk through the water/aid stations along the course. Once I realized that you don't have to run the entire distance, the fear of running a half marathon vanished, instantly. My mind had found a chink in the armor. Once I exploited the weakness of the 13.1 half marathon beast, my mindset changed forever on long distance running. This same technique allowed me to complete a marathon as well. Someone reading this right now is probably saying, "He's probably been running for a long time." I was able to complete three half marathons and one full marathon over the course of a year. I began in May 2016 and completed my third half marathon on April 22, 2017, at the age of 43 with no prior long distance running experience whatsoever. I'm by no means a super athlete, just an average person with high beliefs that I could finish a half marathon. I hope that this encourages you to finish your first half marathon no matter what age you begin at. If I can do it, so can you.

Finishing a 5K or a 10K can be easily accomplished with little or no training at all. If your goal is to run or walk/run a half marathon, then you must tell yourself that you are a runner. You are no longer running for the sake of exercise. You are running to train your body to complete your first half marathon. You are now training for a half marathon.

Many things that I go over in this book are solely my opinion. Every training schedule discussed within this book has been used by me to complete three half marathons and a full marathon. There are several different schools of thought when it comes to how much running per week it takes to train for a half marathon. There are different nutrition guides, shoe strategies, running miles per week, etc. There is, however, one common thing agreed upon by almost all runners - you have to believe in yourself and believe that you are a runner. Without this firmly ingrained in your head, you won't make it past mile nine, and you won't make it to the finish line. I'm not telling you this to discourage you. I'm telling you this to prepare you for the mental battle of running. One week at a time, one day at a time, one mile at a time, and one step at a time will get you to the half marathon finish line.

About the Author

I played sports throughout my youth and even into my adult years. I ran my first 5k at the age of 37 in March of 2008 without any training at all. I finished third place, although my leg muscles felt like I deserved first place. My legs were sore for six days after the race. My next 5k attempt was in 2015 at the age of 42 in my local hometown. I had no intention of placing at all. I ended up running worse than my first 5k by almost two minutes. I placed second with no training at all. I thought I would have learned a lesson by now - nope.

In May 2016, I was flying to Las Vegas for our yearly guys' trip. I was reading a *Sky Mall* magazine, and I came across an article called "Top 100 things to do in Las Vegas." Number eight on the list was run a race through the streets of Las Vegas. During the race, the city blocks off sections of the strip. I was hooked. They offered a 5k, 10k, half marathon and marathon. I liked walking a lot; in fact, one of my favorite things to do in Las Vegas was to see how many steps I could get in a day (my record to date is 42,000). The Rock-and-Roll Half Marathon/Marathon would be taking place in November 2016. I scoured the Internet for any information related to training for a half marathon.

My wife asked me, "Why in the world do you want to run a

half marathon?" I told her because I was physically able to. She said, "You just want to put one of those 13.1 stickers on the back of your car." But truthfully the real reason was much deeper than that. Whenever I catch a fresh dump of powder on my snowboard, there is no other experience like it. I feel like a kid again, and I feel alive. The real reason I wanted to run was because I wanted to feel the accomplishment, feel the pain and feel the glory of crossing the finish line all the while feeling alive. Running allows me to unleash that competitive kid inside me who yearns to feel alive.

Other Books by Scott O. Morton

Beginner to Finisher Series:

Book 1: *Why New Runners Fail: 26 Ultimate Tips You Should Know Before You Start Running!*

Book 2: *5K Fury: 10 Proven Steps to Get You to the Finish Line in 9 weeks or less!*

Book 3: *10K Titan: Push Beyond the 5K in 6 Weeks or Less!*

Book 4: *Beginner's Guide to Half Marathons: A Simple Step-By-Step Solution to Get You to the Finish Line in 12 Weeks!*

Book 5: *Long Run Hacks: 20 Ultimate Tips to Help You Push Through Hard Runs!*

Book 6: *How to Avoid a Half Marathon Meltdown: 10 Things You Need to Know to Make Sure Your First Half Marathon Isn't Your Last!*

Book 7: *Marathon Machine - Breakthrough Your Running Barrier in 18 weeks and Conquer Your Dream! (COMING SOON)*

Supercharge Your Walking Life:

Book 1: *42,000 Steps: 100 simple ways to maximize your daily step count!*

Book 2: *Supercharged Walking: 20 Simple Methods to Help You Level Up Your Stride!*

Book 3: *Walkathon - The Ultimate Guide to Walking a 5K, 10K, Half Marathon, or Marathon!*

FREE BONUS!

SIGN UP TO RECEIVE A FREE 5K, 10K, AND HALF
MARATHON TRAINING SCHEDULE.

BONUS #1
A LOG SHEET TO RECORD YOUR TRAINING!

BONUS #2
A FREE HALF MARATHON PACE PREDICTOR!

http://geni.us/b2fsignup